MEMOIRS,

&c. &c. &c.

THE desolating ravages of death justly claim
the most serious attention at all times, but more
especially when the great and the good become
the victims, and fall under the power of the
King of Terrors. When death enters the pa-
laces of Monarchs and Potentates, it furnishes a
lesson peculiarly humiliating to the pride of man.
It demonstrates that no power or earthly gran-
deur can rescue its possessor from the tomb;
That house, so emphatically described by Job,
as appointed for all living;—And when the good,
those who have been distinguished either in public, or in private life; in the higher or the more
humble classes of society, by their piety, their
acts of benevolence, and the exercise, by divine
aid, of every Christian virtue are called hence,
this also affords a melancholy illustration of St.
Paul's observations, "that sin came into the
world, and death by sin, and that it is appointed
to all men once to die."

The above reflections may be viewed as truly

appropriate, with respect to the lamented decease of His late Royal Highness the Duke of Kent, a Prince combining with Royal dignity the most splendid virtues. Not long since, the nation was called to mourn the death of the amiable Princess Charlotte of Saxe-Cobourg; and the tears of the nation were hardly dried up, ere her illustrious uncle is hurried to the grave.

Edward, Duke of Kent and Strathearn was the fourth son, and fifth child, * of his present Majesty. He was born Nov. 2, 1767. He was distinguished at the juvenile period of his life by an ardent thirst after knowledge, quick perception, a ready capacity, and intellectual powers of a superior nature. While a boy, the conductors of a respectable Literary Journal (The London Magazine) honored Prince Edward, by dedicating to him a volume of their work. After receiving an education worthy of the pre-eminent rank he held in society, and by which he greatly profited, he was sent to Lunenburg to complete his studies, where he resided nearly twelve years. He afterwards went to Hanover, and his inclination leading him to embrace the military profession, he devoted much time to the study of it at that place.

At the age of twenty he was in possession of the command of the Hanoverian guards, with the

* The Princess-Royal of England, now Queen Dowager of Wirtemberg, was born Sept. 29, 1766.

rank of ColoneL. In making the tour of Europe, the Prince remained a considerable time in the city of Geneva; during his residence there, he was appointed, upon the happy recovery of his Royal Father, Colonel of the seventh foot, or Royal Fusileers, in April, 1789, the following year, he returned to England.

The domestic happiness he experienced in the bosom of the Royal Family was limited to a very short period, only ten days being allowed him before he received orders to repair to Gibraltar. It has been said, that during the time his Royal Highness was in Germany, his whole income consisted of an allowance of one thousand pounds per annum, of which his Governor had the sole disposal, except one guinea and a half per week allowed to his Royal Highness for pocket money. General O'Hara was the governor of Gibraltar when the Prince was in the subordinate capacity of Colonel.

Much obloquy has been attached to the Duke's conduct while at Gibraltar: on this subject we subjoin some very judicious observations by a writer of great ability in a popular daily print.*

" His Royal Highness's attention to the appearance and discipline of his regiment was altogether exemplary and unremitting. But as he could not inspire all the military world with an equal sense of the solid value of those dry,

---

* The Times, Tuesday, January 26.

homely, and uninteresting duties which ought to employ so large a portion of military life, or with an equal taste for those *minutia* of the service, of which, nevertheless, when considered in the aggregate, the correct performance adds so much to the precision and efficiency of a military machine, the Colonel of the seventh Fusileers was for some time an unpopular commander. Every military man is not capable of discovering in the best conceived order, or the wisest rule laid down for his observance by superior authority, the direct relation of the means to the end. It may not be thought, at first sight, of serious importance, that an officer's coat, or boot, or pantaloon, should be of a specific fashion, height, or colour; but let us consider that the excellence of an army consists in its susceptibility of collective and uniform impulses, and we must admit that uniformity in smaller things, in homely occupations, and objects of attention—nay, in the form of hats or epaulets, will contribute to enforce upon common minds the main principle of harmony in action. As harmony ought to be the characteristic of every military movement, so the spring of it must be subordination. The Duke of Kent (for the writer of this tribute to his memory was not unacquainted with his professional sentiments) laboured to communicate these two great powers to the troops, for whose qualities he was responsible. He frequently issued orders on points which were of inferior moment, and enforced them vigorously, because he had issued them. By this system, by a conscientious fulfilment of his own duties, a firm requisition of the like propriety from others, and an anxious interposition in behalf of every individual who had wrongs to be redressed, or claims to be recommended, he at length carried the discipline of his regiment to the highest pitch, and established for himself the most respectable military reputation. But in his progress towards this end, he encountered much detraction, considerable obloquy, and some resistance. Complaints were made, which injured his character at home; and mutinies were prepared by the troops, which threatened his authority, and more than once endangered his person."

His Royal Highness having returned to Gibraltar, where he remained in command of the seventh foot, as also of the Queen's Regiment, till June, 1791, when he received orders to sail with his regiment to Quebec, the capital of Canada and of British America, and from thence to Halifax, in Nova Scotia, and afterwards he returned again to Canada. During his service in British America, orders arrived from England for Prince Edward to sail for the West-Indies, he had been prior to this promoted to the rank of a Major-General in the army.

War having commenced between Great Britain

and the Republic of France, Sir Charles Grey, father of Earl Grey, had received instructions to make an attack upon the French West-India islands, his Highness was commanded to join Sir Charles without delay. Great impediments arose, which would have embarrassed a mind less undaunted than Prince Edward's. He had great difficulties to contend with—the navigation of the river Saint Lawrence was closed, and the most extreme danger awaited him in attempting to join the British General, if he passed through the United States. Such perilous circumstances seemed to serve only as a stimulus to excite him to the prompt discharge of the duty imposed upon him; he departed from Quebec, for the purpose of embarking at Boston. The Lake Champlain, which he was forced to pass, was frozen over, and he had the cruel mortification, while travelling over it, to behold two of the sledges in his train, which were laden with his equipage, swallowed up in consequence of the breaking of the ice. Fortunately, upon the Prince's arrival at Boston, an English packet had entered the harbour, on-board of which he entered, and instantly set sail for the West-Indies; danger still awaited him, for some French privateers gave a heavy chase to the packet, which, however, providentially arrived safe at its destined port.

Sir Charles Grey had now commenced the siege of Fort Bourbon, in Martinique. The ene-

my, under General Bellegarde, was strongly en-
trenched on the heights of the Fort. The British
charging with bayonet, and being reinforced by
some troops under General Prescot, the French
commander descended from the heights, and a
sanguinary engagement took place, in which
Prince Edward was eminently distinguished for
his intrepidity—Bellegrade was totally defeated.
Sir Charles, in consequence of his Royal Highness's display of heroism, caused the lower fort to
be designated Fort Edward. His gallantry was
equally conspicuous in the storming of Fort
Royal.

Martinique having surrendered, an attack was
meditated upon St. Lucia; in this expedition, the
command of the brigade of grenadiers was as-
signed to the Prince. In this action his courage
was manifested, " with too little consideration
for his own safety, and too much disregard for
the enemies position. The troops were repuls-
ed; but the Duke of Kent's high personal courage obtained him the applause of the soldiers,
and a flattering rebuke from the Commander-in-
Chief." The British forces afterwards made a
successful attack upon Guadaloupe.

At the close of this brilliant campaign, Prince
Edward returned to Halifax, and in consequence
of his meritorious conduct was nominated Commander of all the forces in Nova Scotia; and, in
1796, he was promoted to the rank of Lieutenant-

General. A new honor now awaited him, for in April, 1799, he was created Duke of Kent and Strathearn, in Great Britain, and Earl of Dublin, in Ireland; and, in the following month, he was appointed General-in-Chief of all the forces in British North America. It has been already stated, that the Duke had sustained a loss when crossing Lake Champlain, his equipage being lost by the ice breaking; another calamity, of a similiar nature, attended his Highness after embarking for America; a transport, containing the whole of the library, maps, furniture, carriages, horses, &c. of the Prince was wrecked in the passage, and all on-board the transport perished. This loss was of a very serious nature, as a great part of his income had been expended in the purchase of the above property, and it has been asserted, that the Duke did not receive any reimbursement.

In his military government at Halifax the Duke of Kent was guided by those ideas, and acted upon that system, which he considered as best calculated to maintain the honor and reputation of the army. He was especially anxious to preclude all irregularities, and to promote a spirit of œconomy. He sedulously directed his attention to the study of military tactics, and the science of fortification, while he preserved the strictest discipline in the army; he also improved the bulwarks of Halifax; and in numerous respects promoted the advantage and welfare of the inhabitants of the province over which he presided. Such was the impression made by his conduct in North America, that the legislative assembly voted five hundred guineas for the purchase of a diamond star, as a token of their veneration and esteem for his character.

The devotedness of the Duke to the duties of his important station, and his indefatigable attention to public business, had a baneful effect upon his constitution, and his health being much impaired, he requested permission to return to England, where he arrived in August, 1800.

In 1802, his Royal Highness was nominated Governor of Gibraltar. At this important garrison "a mass of abuses waited his correcting hand. The establishment of wine-houses, for the sale of liquors to the troops, had been encouraged from shameful motives in those who had the means of suppressing them, and to an extent not more subversive of the health, discipline, and morals of the garrison, than perilous to the safety of the place itself. The Royal Duke, attentive only to the welfare of the community of which he was the head, and scorning the vicious though vast emoluments which some of his predecessors had derived from the sale of licenses for that illegal and ruinous traffic, resolved to cleanse the Augean stable, and to sweep away the abomination of many years. The virtuous attempt was made, but it recoiled upon its author. It is true that the wine-house licenses were withdrawn, that the peaceable inhabitants of Gibraltar could carry on their business, and walk the streets, and repose within their dwellings, at less risk of insult, outrage or robbery, than before; that drunkenness disappeared among the regiments; that cleanliness and discipline were restored, while military punishments were reduced in frequency, the hospitals emptied of their numerous inmates, and the sexton disappointed of his daily work. But we turn to other consequences; the liquor-merchants were forced to discontinue their enormous profits, and instigated the unreflecting soldiery to vengeance for the loss of those indulgencies, which devoured their pay, and destroyed their health. Insubordination broke out on all sides; the reforming Governor was not supported by the local authorities, and he was sacrificed by those nearer home. After receiving the grateful and unanimons acknowledgments of the civil population of Gibraltar, he was recalled from a post in which his efforts for the public good were neither appreciated, nor defended as they ought to have been."

The above judicious observations of an intelligent anonymous writer, will tend to elucidate the unpleasant circumstances which the Duke of Kent was destined to experience in his official character as Governor of Gibralter. No sooner

had he landed at that place, than he observed, with
deep regret, the slovenly appearance of the military assembled on the grand parade. There was
a total want of discipline and order, and if their
appearance on parade was contemptible, their
behaviour and dress when off was infinitely more
so. The peace and tranquillity of the inhabitants
were continually invaded, and offences of a glaring
nature were daily perpetrated. To check such
abuses, to counteract evils of so atrocious a nature, required a mind of Herculean firmness, and
a spirit of undaunted vigour. It required also no
small share of wisdom in the choice of measures
to renovate an abandoned soldiery, whose licentiousness prompted to mutiny.

The ardor of the Duke of Kent was not to be
damped by any difficulties. Having been an
eye-witness of the irregularities so generally
prevalent, he was resolved to lay the axe to
the root of the tree. Coercive measures were
used in vain—the guilty were *punished*, but
not *reclaimed*. Stripes and imprisonment effected no radical change, and as soon as the former
were healed, or the prisoner released, the same
habits of inebriation, of profligacy, and of contu-
macy were resumed. It was necessary to hew
down, to annihilate that infamous system which
was the grand cause of so many evils. His
Royal Highness therefore began the salutary
work of reformation, by rigidly enforcing in-

dustry among the military. It is an adage veri-
fied by every day's experience, that idleness is
the parent of almost every vice. Hence our pri-
sons swarm with offenders against the laws of
their country. Among the military, idleness
generates innumerable evils, gambling, drinking,
and debauchery of every kind. We need only
refer to the period of time when imperial
Rome was sinking into oblivion, that mighty
empire, whose conquering legions had carried
the eagle to the extremities of the globe, to be
convinced of the fatal effects of the want of discipline, and the prevalence of licentiousness in
an army. Habits of industry are difficult to
be acquired by those who are supine and
lethargic; it is necessary that a soldier's time
should be employed;* this essential prelimi-
nary to reform, the Duke of Kent strictly attended to. He established a *roll-call* at sun-
rise, a dress-parade in the middle of the day, and
an undress one, at sun-set.

To stop the progress of drunkenness, he first
diminished the number of wine and liquor-houses,
and then he issued orders which tended to preclude the soldiers from inebriation. He commanded every man to appear before him at meal
hours in a state of sobriety, and as soon as the

* Too much praise cannot be given to the plan introduced by
his Royal Highness the Commander-in-Chief, of evening schools
throughout different regiments.

evening gun was fired, a report was made to him
that every individual soldier was in the barracks.
The Duke also established regimental canteens,
and forbade non-commissioned officers and pri-
vates from frequenting wine-houses; the licenses
of all which houses, in the vicinity of the barracks, were cancelled, and none had their licenses
continued but those situated in the public streets.
The salutary effects of such regulations were soon
apparent; instead of daily and nocturnal scenes
of riot, all was peace, harmony and tranquillity.
The inhabitants, who had so long painfully experienced the horrors of a licentious soldiery,
awoke as it were from a dream, and could scarce-
ly believe such a change had been effected. The
voice of drunken clamour and midnight quarrels
was heard no more, and order was re-established
upon the throne of discord.

The diminution of crimes rendered punishments very rare, and the heart of sensibility was
no longer wounded by spectacles of retributive
justice, which had ceased to occur. In consequence of the regulations above specified, the
garrison was marked as a pattern for exemplary
conduct, regularity, sobriety, and good discipline;
metaphorically speaking—after darkness there
was light.

The conduct of his Royal Highness throughout the whole of this business, was truly patrio-
tic. He cared neither for his personal safety, nor

for his pecuniary interest. He sacrificed them both for the good of the community. Who, but a man of his undaunted mind, would not have been fearful of exciting the revenge of those whose *supposed privileges* he curtailed? Men long indulged in vice are not easily trained to virtue. That his Royal Highness's personal safety was endangered a subsequent passage will sufficiently prove. His *pecuniary interests* were also essentially injured by the decrease of his revenue arising from the wine-house licenses; but having in view the prosperity and the happiness of those under his command, he cared not for the personal inconveniences he sustained.

It may justly be supposed that the privations which the new regulations imposed upon the military, did not fail to excite murmuring and discontent. Some disaffected persons raised a mutiny, which took place Dec. 24, 1802. During this perilous crisis, the Duke betrayed no symptoms of fear, but acted with discreet firmness, in consequence of which the commotion was soon quelled, and the garrison restored to tranquillity. A subsequent dispute took place between the 25th regiment and the Royal Scots, which was productive of no disastrous consequences.

Never was the conduct of a public individual more grossly misrepresented, more vilely calumniated, than that of the Royal Duke: no words were too virulent, no epithets too opprobrious to

lavish upon him. Pens dipped in gall were
made use of to pourtray his character in the
most odious colours; and he was held up to
public odium as the vindictive tyrant of the
army. The force of prejudice, it is well known,
has an overwhelming power. Audi alteram par-
tem—" Hear the other side," is a motto which
justice sanctions, and mercy pleads. In confor-
mity to this equitable adage, the conduct of the
Duke of Kent at Gibraltar should be viewed in
all its bearings. With respect to the general
orders issued by the prince, our readers may
judge of their expediency from the judgment given
of them by a military man of acknowledged
abilities and pre-eminent merit, the late general
Sir William Fawcett. It was the decided opinion of that general, "That no officer in Gibraltar, or in any other garrison, who makes the
exact and regular performance of all the duties
incident to that situation the primary object of
his attention, which he certainly ought to do,
can set up any just and well-founded objections
against it. The pains that the Duke of Kent
must have unavoidably taken in composing so
useful and complete a work, does him infinite
honour. It was, moreover, much wanted, as
garrison-duty, for want of a more general practice
of it in our service, is but very imperfectly
understood and attended to among us. The
Duke of Kent's most meritorious labours, there-

fore, for the benefit and instruction of the army at large, in this important branch of his majesty's service, call for its most grateful and sincere acknowledgements."

After such a proud tribute to the military character of his late Royal Highness the Duke of Kent, who can be so blinded by the force of prejudice as to give credence to those calumnious reports, those ill-founded rumours, which tend to depreciate his fair fame, and tear from his brow the laurels he so justly claimed and received as the reward of merit.

There were not wanting persons resident at Gibraltar, who were eagerly employed in sending to the court of St. James's a distorted and erroneous account of what had taken place. Misrepresentations of the subject were so artfully woven together, that it was absolutely accredited that flagrant impropriety in the conduct of his Royal Highness had caused a general mutiny, in consequence of which the Duke was recalled, upon the alledged basis—" That it was desirable the different departments of government at home, should have the advantage of some personal communication upon the recent events at Gibraltar."

An evident demonstration that his Royal High-ness's conduct was not viewed in that light in which his enemies had placed it, appeared by his being, soon after his return from Gibraltar, elevated to the rank of Field Marshal in the army, which promotion took place on September 5th, 1806.

In 1807, the public attention was engaged by a singular prosecution exhibited by Colonel Wardle against his Royal Highness the Duke of York, Commander-in-chief. The subject of the charges brought forward related to a supposed influence which Mrs. Clarke, a celebrated courtezan, had over the Royal Duke; Captain Dodd was at this time private secretary to the Duke of Kent, and it being ascertained that the secretary had some knowledge of that female, a general rumour prevailed that the Duke of Kent was implicated in the affair. Such a charge was repelled with no small indignation by his Royal Highness in private, in an interview with Colonel Dodd, in the presence of Lord Harrington, and in public in the House of Peers, and he exonerated himself from so foul an aspersion.

The embarrassed circumstances of his Royal Highness induced him, after fruitless endeavours to have his finances recruited, to leave this country and retire to Brussels, where an immense number of English had taken up their abode. During his absence in the year 1816, a proposition was made for celebrating his birth-day on the second of November in that year. In consequence of this, a meeting was held, at which the following

B 2

address was voted and transmitted to his Royal Highness :

"Sir,—We the assembled members of various benevolent institutions, honoured with the patronage of your Royal Highness, being desirous of publicly marking our attachment to your person, and our just appreciation of your virtues and talents, beg permission to tender you the sincere tribute of our respect and affection.

"We are induced, by every social and moral principle, to pay peculiar honour to a dynasty distinguished like that of your illustrious family, for its paternal protection of every interest of knowledge and humanity. What then must we not owe to your Royal Highness, for the conspicuous part you have taken in the benign spirit of the House of Brunswick; by your unwearied and powerful exertions to render effective those measures which constitute the glory of Great Britain ; and which, embracing every class of society at home, providing for the impoverished, relieving the diseased, and instructing the ignorant, aim at extending their blessings over the whole earth : we are satisfied, that in offering to your Royal Highness the gratitude of our hearts, we are also speaking in the name of our country, and we are proud of an opportunity of expressing, in the language of truth, sentiments which are re-echoed among all ranks of the British empire.

" Signed, on behalf of the stewards and friends
of the Meeting,

MATTHEW WOOD, Mayor, and Chairman.

JAMES THOMPSON, Honorary Secretary.

The first celebration of so joyous a day, when
an altar of gratitude was erected to the Prince
of philanthrophy, took place on the anniversary
of his birth; his illustrious brother, the Duke
of Sussex, was in the chair, and was supported by
the Right Honourable Matthew Wood, Lord-
mayor, and William Smith, Esq. M. P. for the
City of Norwich. Of the numerous toasts
given at this festival, (which was held at Fish-
monger's-hall, Upper Thames-street,) the following was received with the most enthusiastic and
universal shouts of applause:—

" May every royal duke in Europe, qualify himself for the same truly noble return, as his Royal
Highness the Duke of Kent, from the great body
of his fellow-subjects."

Upon this memorable occasion, many respectable persons were present, and amongst
others, his Serene Highness the Duke of Orleans,
an illustrious emigrant ;* who made a concise but
energetic speech, which evinced the interest
he took in the meeting, and what a high opinion

* The Duke of Orleans was the son of the infamous Egalite !
His Highness for sometime exercised the humble office of a school-
master in this country.

he entertained of the Duke of Kent. The Duke of Sussex, upon the health of his royal brother being drank, in a speech at once appropriate and truly impressive, expatiated upon the character of his dear relative:—" That illustrious person," said he, " was as anxious to shun praise as he was zealous to deserve it." What an eulogium !

The Duke of Kent's health was given by the chief magistrate in the following manner :—

" The Duke of Kent, the patron of charity— the promoter of education—the ornament of his country—and the friend of the human race."

A state of celibacy is in no respect congenial to a social disposition ; the Duke of Kent found a *vacuum* even amidst his active duties as a man, a christian, and a philanthropist. He looked around the Protestant courts of Europe, to find a helpmate for him in the person of some amiable and accomplished princess; at length his affections were placed on her serene Highness Victoria Maria Louisa, youngest daughter of his late Serene Highness Francis Frederic Anthony Resguiry, Duke of Saxe-Cobourg, of Saalfield. The happy coincidence of temper and disposition, congruity of ideas, harmony of opinion, and feelings of benevolence, which distinguished both parties, led to a matrimonial union, which was solemnized, first at Cobourg,

May 29, 1818, and afterwards at Kew, on the 11th of July following.

The Duchess of Kent was a widow, having been married to the Hereditary Prince of Leiningen, by whom she had two children, one now living with her, the Princess Fodor. The conjugal felicity which his Royal Highness enjoyed in his union with his amiable Duchess was augmented by the happy event of the birth of a daughter, which event took place at Kensington-palace, May 24, 1819. Her Royal Highness was on the continent, until an advanced period of her pregnancy; the Duke, anxious that her accouchement should take place at home, had her removed by gentle stages to Calais, from whence, in April, she embarked for England, and landed at Dover. In their progress to Kensington-palace, the Duke and Duchess honoured Lord Darnley with a visit at Cobham-hall.

In addition to Doctor Davis and Doctor Wilson, who attended the Duchess as accoucheurs, the singular circumstance occurred of a *female doctor* attending her Royal Highness, namely, Dr. Charlotte Von Siebold, * the daughter of an eminent German physician, who, after attending

---

* A learned German lady, Anne Marie Shurman, celebrated for her knowledge of the learned languages, received the degrees of L.L.D., M.D. &c.

a regular series of academical lectures, and passing her examination with singular honor, received a diploma.

The embarrassments of the Duke of Kent having greatly increased, a proposal was submitted to parliament, by Mr. Alderman Wood, for the disposal of his effects by way of Lottery, for the liquidation of his debts ; a warm debate ensued, in which Lord Castlereagh forcibly pointed out the degrading impropriety of such a measure, which of course was abandoned. The infant Princess was baptised at Kensington-palace, by the names of Alexandrina Victoria.

At the close of the autumn of the last year his Royal Highness engaged a house at Sidmouth, in Devonshire, to which place he, his amiable Duchess, the infant Princess, and the Princess Fodor, repaired ; his Royal Highness was greeted during his journey in the most flattering manner, and, on his arrival at Sidmouth, was hailed by a general illumination. The delectable and romantic scenery, in the vicinity of that fashionable and elegant place of resort, enchanted his Royal Highness.

Not long after the arrival of these illustrious personages in Devonshire, a circumstance occurred, which although of a trivial nature, might have been attended with the most serious consequences.

An apprentice boy, aping his superiors, had

equipped himself with a gun, and considered himself a true Devon sportsman, when unfortunately, as he was playing with the tube of death, a chance shot broke the windows of the royal nursery, and passed very near the infant princess, then in the arms of her nurse. The alarm having subsided, the rash and foolish youth was apprehended for his culpable conduct; but the Duke of Kent, with his accustomed good nature, ordered him to be discharged on condition of his promising to abandon that species of field sports.

The fascinating scenery which Sidmouth presented to the view of the Duke of Kent, occasioned him to make occasional perambulations in its vicinity. It was in one of those excursions, that this amiable and illustrious personage met with the ostensible cause of his death; after his Royal Highness had been taking one of his usual walks, accompanied by Captain Conroy, it was found that the wet had penetrated through his boots: in vain did Dr. Wilson urge him to take a medicine to repel the attack of indisposition, so frequently the consequence of wet feet. His highness, engaged with the infant caresses of the young Princess, treated this salutary and sound advice with a degree of nonchalance, arising from a too sanguine opinion of the strength of his constitution, and declined taking the medicine. Alas! this was the prelude to that fatal event which has bathed the nation in tears.

A few days only had elapsed, 'ere symptoms of indisposition appeared, which soon assumed so alarming an appearance as to occasion daily bulletins of his health to be published.   To those best acquainted with the constitution of the Royal Duke, fearful forebodings were entertained of the result of the illness with which he was afflicted.   His disorder was at times vacilating, until the lungs became inflamed; the utmost alarm now prevailed, and the physician, (Dr. Maton, of Spring-gardens,) being called in, through the medium of the bulletins, communicated to the public their suspicion of his return to a state of convalescence.   From this time no hope was entertained, and his Royal Highness was apprized of his imminent danger ; he received the intelligence with pious resignation, and expired in the arms of his beloved Duchess, in the very act of faintly articulating prayers for her future felicity.   This melancholy event occurred at ten o'clock, A. M. on Sunday, January 23, 1820.

In the preceding Memoir of Field-Marshal Edward Duke of Kent, we have chiefly viewed his character in a military point of view : we shall now take a general survey of it.   One of the most prominent traits which distinguished the late Duke of Kent, was a spirit indefatigable in ameliorating the sorrows of humanity.   He verily went about doing good.   And like the

Emperor Titus Vespasian, who was the delight
of mankind, he accounted every day lost in which
he had not performed a benevolent action.

Amidst innumerable anecdotes upon record
of his private benevolence, the following is peculiarly worthy of notice. While resident at Gibraltar, a soldier had a boat, in which, when off
duty, he employed himself in fishing. One
night, when at sea with his eldest boy behind the
rock, a Levant gale came on, and they both
perished. His widow was far advanced in pregnancy, and this sad event plunged her into the
deepest affliction. A subscription was set on
foot for her benefit, and the third night after the
catastrophe, while she was sitting weeping and
bemoaning her cruel fate, a gentleman sud-
denly appeared, who made the kindest enquiries
as to her situation. He took the children on
his knee and kissed them, consoled her, bid her
dry up her tears, and putting twelve gold pieces
into her hand (cobs, or dollars of gold, current at
Gibraltar) instantly departed. The following day
he called again, and repeated his visits for several
days successively. When her time drew near
he sent a doctor to attend her, and provided every
article requisite for her comfort. The woman was
filled with astonishment at the exalted benevolence of her unknown benefactor. She remained
ignorant of the rank of the person who had thus
befriended her, until some weeks after her de-

livery, when, being at a review, she recognised, in the person of the Duke of Kent, her hitherto unknown benefactor. A day or two after, the duke called again, but her eldest boy having mentioned his name, he never called more, but continued to send regular supplies of money to the widow.

The *public* philanthropy of his Royal Highness was unbounded ; to enumerate all the charities of which he was either a patron or a liberal subscriber, would be to mention nearly all the benevolent institutions which are to be met with in this great metropolis and its environs. To the following philanthropic establishments he was a distinguished benefactor.

Society for Educating and Clothing poor SONS OF THE CLERGY.

Society for Propagating the GOSPEL in the Highlands and Islands of Scotland.

THE AFRICAN SOCIETY, for promoting Christian Knowledge among the Africans.

The WESTMINSTER INFIRMARY.

BRITISH SCHOOLS OF EDUCATION, founded by Joseph Lancaster.

BRITISH SCHOOL OF INDUSTRY, Islington.

LYING-IN CHARITY for delivering poor Women at their own Habitations.

LONDON TRUSS SOCIETY.

UNIVERSAL DISPENSARY FOR CHILDREN.

ROYAL HUMANE SOCIETY.

St. Anne's Society Schools, Aldersgate.

The Caledonian Asylum.

Benevolent Society of St. Patrick.

Society for the Relief of Widows and Orphans of Medical Men.

London Society for the Conversion of the Jews. His Royal Highness laid the first stone of the Jewish Episcopal Chapel erected by that society.

The British and Foreign Bible Society.

The Literary Fund for the Relief of distressed Authors.

Society for the Relief of distressed Artists.

The Philanthropic Harmonists.

The Mile-End Philanthropic Society, for the Relief of Persons imprisoned for Small Debts.

The City Dispensary.

The Finsbury Dispensary, &c. &c.

His Royal Highness was also Vice President of the Veterinary College; and of the the Philosophical Society of London.

The Duke of Kent was a great encourager of literature, and many works of great merit were published under his immediate patronage.

Mr. Owen of Lanark owes much to the zealous exertions he made for bringing into action that gentleman's plans for ameliorating the distresses of the poor, and for educating their offspring. Unabated was his attention to this subject, even to a short period before he retired to Sidmouth. He attended a committee of Mr. Owen's friends at the City of London Tavern, on July 27th, 1819, having also attended a former one, held at Free-Mason's Hall, on June 26th of the same year.

In his theological principles, although a professed member of the established church, he was peculiarly liberal in his sentiments ; and acting upon such principles, he occasionally, for the service of public charities, attended chapels not in the establishment. For the Humane Society he attended at Salter's Hall Meeting-House, at Hanover Chapel, Peckham, and at the Scotch Church in Well Street, Oxford Road, at each of which places the sermon was preached by the Rev. Dr. Collyer. The Rev. Rowland Hill preached a sermon before him at Surry Chapel, in behalf of the British and Foreign Schools of Education. In the choice of his chaplains he exercised great discrimination ; without enumerating the names of other reverend gentlemen who were appointed to this office, those of the Rev. G. H. White, Rev. Leigh Richmond, and Rev. Dr. Rudge, are sufficient to mark his sense of piety and talents in that respect.

The manners of his Royal Highness were

Ingram Content Group UK Ltd.
Milton Keynes UK
UKHW050613310323
419329UK00022B/38

9 780343 371920